Working Horses

Police Horses

by Rachel Grack

Bullfrog Books

Ideas for Parents and Teachers

Bullfrog Books let children practice reading informational text at the earliest reading levels. Repetition, familiar words, and photo labels support early readers.

Before Reading
- Discuss the cover photo. What does it tell them?
- Look at the picture glossary together. Read and discuss the words.

Read the Book
- "Walk" through the book and look at the photos. Let the child ask questions. Point out the photo labels.
- Read the book to the child, or have him or her read independently.

After Reading
- Prompt the child to think more. Ask: Police horses help in many situations. Why do some police officers use horses?

Bullfrog Books are published by Jump!
5357 Penn Avenue South
Minneapolis, MN 55419
www.jumplibrary.com

Library of Congress Cataloging-in-Publication Data is available at www.loc.gov or upon request from the publisher.

ISBN: 979-8-88524-496-1 (hardcover)
ISBN: 979-8-88524-497-8 (paperback)
ISBN: 979-8-88524-498-5 (ebook)

Editor: Katie Chanez
Designer: Molly Ballanger

Photo Credits: L T/Dreamstime, cover; David Tran/iStock, 1; Jimmy Ostgard/Dreamstime, 3; Sean Pavone/Shutterstock, 4; imageBROKER/Alamy, 5; dpa picture alliance/Alamy, 6–7, 23br; Roberto Galan/iStock, 8; Tim Fleming/Alamy, 9; eddtoro/Shutterstock, 10–11, 23tl; e X p o s e/Shutterstock, 12–13; 4kclips/Shutterstock, 14–15; Jeff Greenberg/age fotostock/SuperStock, 16; Spondylolithesis/iStock, 17, 22bl; Melissa Lyttle/The Tampa Bay Times/AP Images, 18–19; Allison Bailey/Alamy, 20–21; jimplumb/iStock, 22tl; spatuletail/Shutterstock, 22tr; Sheila Fitzgerald/Shutterstock, 22br, 23tr; acceptphoto/Shutterstock, 23bl; A-Shropshire-Lad/iStock, 24.

Printed in the United States of America at Corporate Graphics in North Mankato, Minnesota.

Table of Contents

Helping People

The city is busy.

Police horses walk by.

They help keep people safe.

They work with police officers.

police officer

Officers train the horses.

The horses hear loud noises.

Things touch them.

They learn to stay calm.

Horses are tall.
Officers sit in
saddles.

saddle

They can see over people.

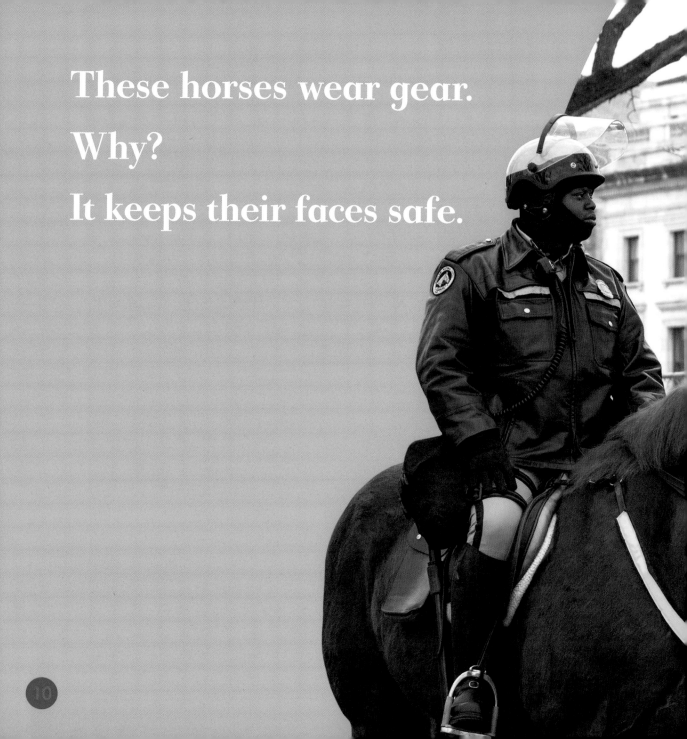

These horses wear gear.
Why?
It keeps their faces safe.

visor

nose guard

U.S. PARK POLICE

There is a parade.

Horses help.

They keep people off the road.

Horses are big.
They stop a crowd.

crowd

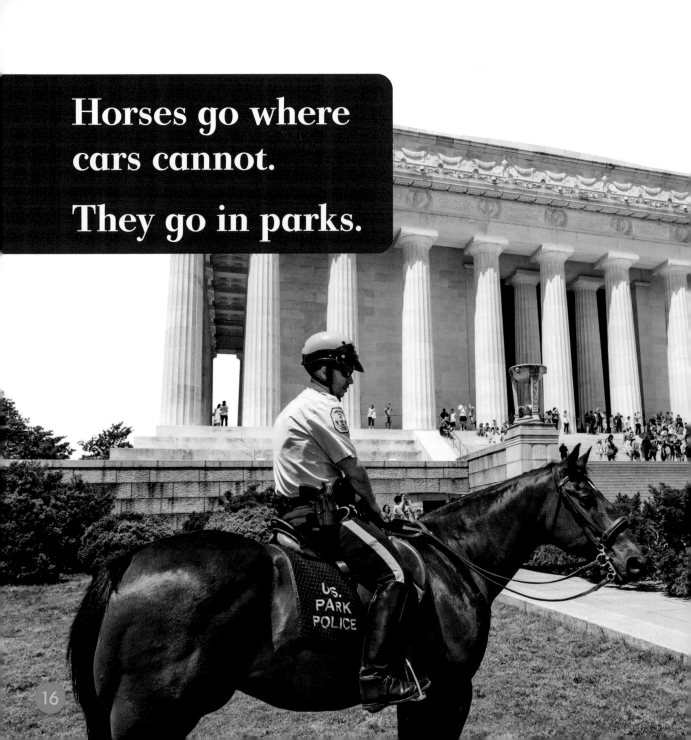

Horses go where cars cannot.

They go in parks.

Someone is lost on a hike.

Horses help officers look for them.

Today, we meet
police horses.

They are friendly.

We pet them.

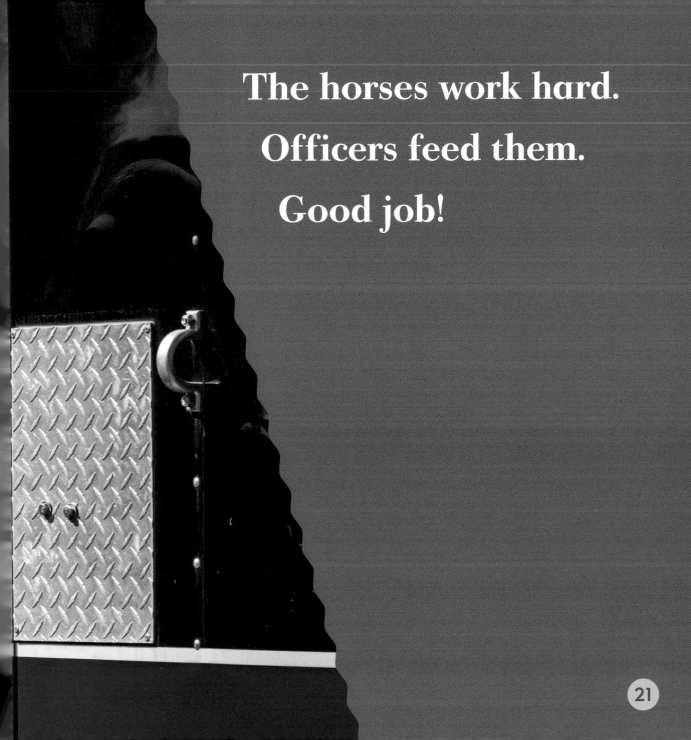

The horses work hard.
Officers feed them.
Good job!

On the Job

Police horses have many jobs. Take a look at some of them!

crowd control
These horses stop a crowd from going somewhere. They also break up crowds.

patrol
These horses carry police officers on the streets. They make sure people are safe.

search and rescue
These horses help officers look for people who are lost or in danger.

special events
These horses march in parades. They may meet people in the community.

gear
Safety equipment.

parade
A march of people or vehicles to mark a celebration or event.

saddles
Seats for riders that are strapped

train
To teach an animal how to

Index

To Learn More

Finding more information is as easy as 1, 2, 3.

❶ Go to www.factsurfer.com

❷ Enter "policehorses" into the search box.

❸ Choose your book to see a list of websites.